FOLKLORE KEEPS THE PAST ALIVE

FOLKLORE

KEEPS

the

PAST

ALIVE

ARTHUR PALMER HUDSON

EUGENIA DOROTHY BLOUNT LAMAR
MEMORIAL LECTURES, 1961

Delivered at Mercer University on October 24, 25, 26

UNIVERSITY OF GEORGIA PRESS

ATHENS

784. 4973
H 86 f

45,072

Contents

Foreword

IN AN EARLY AMERICAN SONG THERE IS THE INTERESTING boast that every Kentuckian was "half a horse and half an alligator." Arthur Palmer Hudson is a man of many parts, and he could hardly be limited to such a bipartite classification as the one above. First of all, Dr. Hudson is a consummate folklorist, at home among the entangled fields of the folksong, folksay, tall tale, and all the rest. Also, he is a longtime student of English and American literature, and spices his references to folklore with singularly appropriate allusions to a wide range of literature. Despite his long familiarity with these materials, he approaches all his scholarly interests with the enthusiasm of the neophyte. His remarkable memory enables him to talk at length on a variety of subjects; and he is never unwilling to share his knowledge with others. As the fifth speaker in the Lamar series, Dr. Hudson brought to the campus of Mercer University a personal charm and warmth of personality that will not soon be forgotten.

With the publication of this fifth series of Eugenia Dorothy Blount Lamar Memorial Lectures, delivered at Mercer University in October 1961, the Lamar Lecture Committee and the University reaffirm their gratitude to the late Mrs. Lamar's wisdom and generosity in endowing this perpetual series of lectures. Mrs. Lamar, a cultural leader in Macon and the South for nearly three-quarters of a century, was keenly interested in the continuation of traditional Southern values amid the kaleidoscope of social and economic changes taking place in the modern South. She left a legacy to Mercer University with the request that it be used "to provide lectures of the very highest type of scholarship which will aid in the permanent preservation of the values of Southern culture, history, and literature."

BENJAMIN W. GRIFFITH, JR., *Chairman*
The Lamar Lecture Committee

Mercer University
Macon, Georgia

LECTURE

ONE

The Poetry of Earth: Two Old Folksongs

ON A WINTER EVENING IN 1816, THE TWENTY-ONE-YEAR-OLD John Keats and Leigh Hunt composed, "in friendly rivalry," their sonnets "On the Grasshopper and Cricket." According to their mutual friend Charles Cowden Clarke, who refereed the contest, Keats "won as to time," and the generous Hunt showed "a sincere look of pleasure at the first line—'The poetry of earth is never dead.' 'Such a prosperous beginning,' he said." It is not one of Keats's best sonnets, but, like most of the things he wrote even when very young, it has his touch of genius in it, and it is pleasing.

> The poetry of earth is never dead:
>   When all the birds are faint with the hot sun,
>   And hide in cooling trees, a voice will run
> From hedge to hedge about the new-mown mead;
> That is the Grasshopper's—he takes the lead
>   In summer luxury,—he has never done
>   With his delights; for when tired out with fun
> He rests at ease beneath some pleasant weed.

1

The poetry of earth is ceasing never:
  On a lone winter evening, when the frost
    Has wrought a silence, from the stove there shrills
The Cricket's song, in warmth increasing ever,
  And seems to one in drowsiness half lost,
    The Grasshopper's among some grassy hills.

Here Keats is of course writing about the immemorial
and invincible beauty of earth. He said that "A thing of
beauty is a joy for ever." And he exhibited that beauty in
a thousand felicitous lines and epithets scattered through
his poetry. But he was equally sensitive to the haunting
beauty of an old song, like "La Belle Dame sans Merci,"
or an old tale, like that which is the foursquare, solid
structure of "The Eve of St. Agnes."

There are two old songs—one that has haunted me since
my boyhood, the other an old lullaby that has recently
come to my attention and haunts me also—which exhibit
the poetry of earth that we hope will never die.

Sixty years ago, as a boy in Attala County, Mississippi,
I heard literally the pipes of Pan, perhaps the oldest kind
of music made by man in his brief time in this world. Of
course, I did not then recognize its nature and antiquity.
But now I believe I do.

The music comes mainly on long, lazy summer days,
but never entirely lacking at any season or hour, around
sundown, from the fields along the creeks and little
branches where young rabbits were flashing their white
cottontails around the bends; from bare hilltops mounted
by saddlebag loghouses and flanked by lonely uplands;
from cribs and cotton pens; from little shelves on the
creek banks where fishermen drowsily watched their corks;
from the pasture paths where the young'uns were driving
the cows home for the milking; from cabins with the
smoke of supper fires spiraling up into the still and rosy
air and the aroma of parching coffee and the groan of the

grinding mills emanating therefrom; above the lows of the cattle, the brays of the mules, the caws of crows on their weary way to roost, the crows of cocks, and the pot-racks of guinea fowls, and at dusk the first tentative prelude of the katydid symphony—doming and interpenetrating all these sounds and signs of life in earth and sky and man and beast—a fretwork of melody, like silver threads, bound all together.

This was the monotonous but never oppressive music of Negro boys playing on homemade flutes and pipes. It might almost have been the voice of the landscape, like the Highland reaper's song under a different and austerer sky. The summertime was best for the melody, when all things that loved the sun (and some who in that clime loathed its beating on bent and toiling backs), but loved more the sundown and "quitting time," were out of doors. But all seasons and most of the hours were propitious for such music, and it was ever gay and grave, lonesome and sweet.

So it seems to a transplanted countryman from Attala, in the nostalgia of sixty-nine years of age.

The instruments on which the boys fluted or piped were constructed from the bamboo canes that grew (beyond the reach of winter-browsing cattle), fifteen to thirty feet high (making fine fishing poles also), along the fertile banks of the as-yet-unchoked creeks and in old meandering stream beds too wet to cultivate. With a Barlow knife a boy patiently and painfully whittled down a large cane with joints ten to fifteen inches long and an inch or an inch-and-a-quarter in diameter. One of the longest, largest, and straightest joints he cut off, leaving the natural plug at the larger end and cutting it off just below the next plug. At the plug end he burnt and bored a rather large blow-hole, usually with a red-hot rod; at the open end, with a nail set in a corncob, he bored the finger-holes, five in number.

When the job was finished and the cane was dried (though he didn't have to wait until it was, and usually didn't), he had a flute—and a pretty good one too.

A few boys made pipes by cutting five smaller cane joints of varying length and size, to give the proper pitch, leaving one end of each open, binding them together in a row with the open ends even, backing them with flattened hickory bark or a thin shingle butt, and cementing the whole together with wads of sweetgum or pine rosin (both also good for chewing and keeping the lips moist), scraped from the handiest axe-hacked or axle-scraped tree.

The boys made these flutes and pipes and learned to play them, from one another. So far as I knew (and we had several rounds of flute-makers and -players on my father's and surrounding farms over a period of at least fifteen years during which I noticed things), they had no instruction in either art from their elders. They made and played them as spontaneously as they played marbles and mumblepeg and, in a few instances, as they shot craps. I am absolutely certain that they never learned such things from the books and/or formal instruction of the old-field, grass-chimneyed schools; very few of them ever attended any school or learned even the rudiments of reading and writing in any way. I never heard of any flute-playing at Negro churches. I am fairly certain that I never saw a store-bought flute in Attala County before I left it at the age of twenty. So far as I remember, flutes were not then advertised or pictured in the Sears, Roebuck and Montgomery Ward mail-order catalogues or county newspaper. The prototypes of the present-day hillbilly bands, which played for square dances, did not use flutes or pipes.

In making playthings such as these, and little wagons with native-oak frames and running-gear cut from green poles, and wheels from thin crosswise-sawed slices of large and round logs (usually blackgum), and yokes and hickory-bark-plaited whips for the bull yearlings they trained to pull their juggernauts, and "fluttermills" for the dammed-up little spring branches, and blowguns, and slingshots, and bows and arrows, the Negro boys usually showed more mechanical ingenuity and manual dexterity than did white boys of comparable age. Wiley and little Sam, sons of black sharecropper Sam Baity, always outdid my brother and me; only the tow-headed, blue-eyed pure Anglo-Saxon Hodges boys across the road from us on the old Brister place could beat them as artificers.

Where and how did these Negro boys learn to make and play flutes and pipes? Had the instruments and the art of playing them been imported from Africa by the boys' slave ancestors, or by their grandfathers and great-grandfathers from the more "civilized" Carolinas and Virginia and Georgia, where men did play flutes (as witness Sidney Lanier, flautist in a Baltimore orchestra)? How far back in American history do the records go of cane-flute playing by Negroes or by anybody else? Are there any records at all? I don't know. I don't know anyone who does know.

So with the bullroarer, instrument of sonic torture. So with the dumb-bull, made by stretching a 'possum pelt or a cowhide over the cut of a hollow, thin-walled log, letting it dry hard and taut, then affixing the end of a knotted string in the middle of the head and rosining the string. A boy "played" it by drawing the string between thumb and forefinger, and it made an awful racket. The Negro boys (and the whites too) also made bark whistles from willow or hickory finger-size sprouts and saplings. Next to the flutes and pipes in musical capacity were the cornstalk fiddles with rosin bows. About these there was a jingle—

> Cornstalk fiddle and rosin bow
> Makes gals dance wherever you go.

Where and from whom did these boys learn to make
and play such instruments? The melodies played on flutes
and pipes may be more easily explained. They were quite
simple; even I learned to whistle or hum some of them,
in spite of being completely unversed in musicology and
as totally illiterate in music as the Negro boys were.

Yet a few of the tunes played by the Negro boys I recog-
nized as corresponding to those of current simple songs
like "Old Dan Tucker" and "Go Tell Aunt Nancy [or
Patsy] Her Old Gray Goose Is Dead." Another, taught me
by my father, runs:

> Jaybird settin' on a swingin' limb,
> He wunk at me, I wunk at him;
> Cocked my gun an' split his chin,
> An' lef' the arrer stickin' in.

A small number of the boys, the older and more sophisticated ones, sometimes sang a little song while the flautist
or piper played.

Only one of these do I clearly remember. The tune I
recall sharply; the name I remember as "The Holly Bluff."
The Negro boys from whom I learned the song didn't call
it anything—they just played it, and a few sang it—perhaps
never thinking of a song as having a title.

Whatever the boys may or may not have owed to African
music, or whatever may have been the song's primitive relationship to Greek (or any other kind of European) song,
it certainly shared a theme with Theocritus and David
and Solomon.

The music is "long measure," one of the two most
common ballad patterns, easily wedded to words for a
song. I guarantee that it is as genuine a folksong as William Butler Yeats's "Down by the Sally Gardens," the tune
and a few lines of which he said he got from an old Dublin
washerwoman, or John Jacob Niles's "I Wonder as I

Wander," which he claimed he got from a girl gospel singer at Murphy, North Carolina. I only wish the Mississippi tune were as exquisite, and the words were as lovely, as those of either song.

THE HOLLY BLUFF

WAY DOWN BY THE HOL-LY BLUFF, MET A GAL BY THE
COT-TON GIN, GIVE HER 'SIM-MONS AN' KISS-ES E-NOUGH,
BUT SHE WOULD-N' KISS ME A-G'IN.

Way down by the holly bluff
    Met a gal by the cotton gin,
Give her 'simmons an' kisses enough,
    But she wouldn' kiss me ag'in.

Way down on the holly bluff
    Saw that gal by the hog-hangin' pole,
Give her candy an' a bottle o' snuff,
    But she wouldn' give me no ham or jowl.

Way down under the holly bluff
    Set with the gal by the washin' hole,
Messed up her dress an' treated her rough,
    But she wouldn' give me no jelly roll.

Whatever the relation of this song to the Song of Solomon or *The Greek Anthology* or the Theocritean tradition, the boy and the girl were feeling the emotions vibrant in men and women in the vineyards of Engedi, in Tempe, or in the dales of Arcady.

They were doing the same thing (at least the boy was) as the lovers forever young on the Attic shape. Here, as surely as in the Bishop's specification for the frieze of his tomb, the Mississippi Negro youth is "one Pan/Ready to twitch the Nymph's last garment off." Here, too, far above all breathing human passion, their love remains forever unconsummated, suspended in a dreamy tune and snatch of song on the tenuous thread of an old man's memory.

Let Malvolios and other self-appointed moralists who may object to this song, or at least one word in it, listen to the singing of the lovely English pastoral "The Nightingale," with suspicions aroused and wits sharpened to detect its *double-entendres,* and then only try to find any published critical objection to the song on grounds of taste. The English and Europeans slip such things over much more deftly than we (and our Mississippi Muse) can manage.

Negro boys in Attala County, Mississippi, half a century ago were playing and singing tunes and songs like that. What are they playing and singing today, with their electric guitars, radios, TVs, and phonograph records? Are they much better now at this sort of things than the white boys? Who can tell what either whites or blacks or both may do? Who, in 1900 or even 1912, could have prophesied William Alexander Percy, and Eudora Welty, and William Faulkner?

Looking to the possibility that a thermonuclear blast might wither forever the vineyards of Engedi, the dales of Tempe and of Arcady, and the valleys of Mississippi alike, and silence alike the silver flutes of Greece and the cane flutes of Yoknapatawpha and Attala, Mr. Faulkner in his Nobel prize acceptance speech said, "I believe that

man will prevail." Nearly one hundred fifty years before
Faulkner, a greater poet, facing his world in ruins, wrote,
"The poetry of earth is never dead." If it is not heard in
the summer song of the grasshopper and the winter chirp
of the cricket or in homemade cane flutes of black boys,
it will be heard in some other equally unmistakable and
unforgettable key.

Perry Merry Dictum Domini

The first version of this old lullaby-riddle is from Mrs.
Edward E. Lanphere of Chapel Hill, North Carolina. Mrs.
Lanphere has lived in various regions of the United
States, but she is sure that she learned the lullaby-riddle
from her father during her childhood, around sixty years
ago, in Nebraska.

Mrs. Lanphere's father, Joseph Downing, a country doc-
tor in Nebraska, sang it to her as a monotonous "go-to-
sleepy" lullaby when she was a baby, and later when she
was a little girl and accompanied him on long calls on the
Nebraska prairie. Dr. Downing, she says, was born in
Illinois in 1856, of a family that had bought a thousand
acres of rich Illinois land for a dollar an acre and moved
from Loudoun County, Virginia, to the new state. He told
his daughter that he learned the lullaby-riddle from his
father, in early childhood. Mrs. Lanphere believes, then,
that it was traditional in the Downing family before the
removal from Virginia.

"Perry Merry Dictum Domini" was sung in my presence
and tape-recorded by me on February 19, 1961, at Chapel
Hill, North Carolina. The text has been authenticated in
conversation with Mrs. Lanphere. The notation of the
tune was made by Mrs. Mary Frances Odum Schinhan
from the singing of Mrs. Lanphere and has been carefully
authenticated.

1. I had four brothers over the sea.
       Perry merry dictum domini.
    They each brought a present unto me.
       Perry merry dictum domini.
       Partem quantum perry merry centum.
       Perry merry dictum domini.

2. The first brought a coat without any thread.
       Perry merry dictum domini.
    The second brought a book that couldn't be read.
       Perry merry dictum domini, etc.

3. The third brought a cherry without any stone.
       Perry merry dictum domini.
    The fourth brought a chicken without any bone.
       Perry merry dictum domini, etc.

4. What kind of coat doesn't have any thread?
       Perry merry dictum domini.
    What kind of book cannot be read?
       Perry merry dictum domini.

5. How can a cherry have no stone?
       Perry merry dictum domini.
    How can a chicken have no bone?
       Perry merry dictum domini, etc.

6. A sheepskin coat's without a thread.
       Perry merry dictum domini.
    A book in type cannot be read.
       Perry merry dictum domini, etc.

7. A cherry in blossom has no stone.
  Perry merry dictum domini.
 A chicken in the egg doesn't have any bone.
  Perry merry dictum domini.
  Partem quantum perry merry centum.
  Perry merry dictum domini.

This song has all the parts of the fully developed riddle except the penalty or forfeit—introduction, description, challenge, and (instead of penalty or forfeit) solution. As in "Riddles Wisely Expounded," the riddles are arranged in pairs, all of them being given without interruption by solution, and answered in order. The last two are identical with two in "Captain Wedderburn's Courtship," "chicken" being substituted for "capon." The better-known "Riddle Song" has "chicken," and the answer is usually "a chicken when it's pippin'."

Once, in conversation with her friend and teacher the late Louise Pound, distinguished philologian and folklorist of the University of Nebraska, Mrs. Lanphere remarked that she knew an old lullaby-riddle sung to her by her father, and sang and quoted "Perry Merry Dictum Domini" to Miss Pound. Miss Pound commented that, so far as she knew, Mrs. Lanphere was the only American who had been reported as knowing it, except Woodrow Wilson, who was said to have sung it to his children.

In the *Saturday Evening Post* for November 14, 1936, appeared the first of a series of autobiographical articles by Eleanor Wilson McAdoo with Margaret Y. Gaffey, "The Wilsons: Princeton Days." Writing of the Wilson family life while the children were small, Eleanor Wilson McAdoo recalled:

After prayers, lights went out. Margaret and Jessie had learned, after one brief struggle, that they must go quietly to sleep alone in the dark. Father and mother bore my heart-broken sobbing for some time and then acknowledged themselves defeated. I was sung to and cuddled, and the others benefited by my wickedness, for it gave us the most enchanting memory of our childhood—father sitting on the nursery floor singing Sweet and Low, Watchman, Tell Us of the Night, and a lullaby I have never heard since.

> *I had four brothers over the sea,*
> *Peri Meri Dictum Domini.*
> *They each sent a present unto me,*
> *Partum Quartum Peri Meri Centum*
> *Peri Meri Dictum Domini.*

> *The first brought a cherry without any stone—*
> *Chorus—*
> *The second brought a chicken without any bones,*
> *Chorus—*

> *The third brought a blanket without any thread,*
> *Chorus—*
> *The fourth brought a book that couldn't be read,*
> *Chorus—*

> *When a cherry's in bloom, it hasn't any stones,*
> *Chorus—*
> *When a chicken's in the egg, it hasn't any bones,*
> *Chorus—*

> *When a blanket's in the loom, it hasn't any thread,*
> *Chorus—*
> *When a book's in the press, it cannot be read,*
> *Chorus—*
> *Partum Quartum Peri Meri Centum*
> *Peri Meri Dictum Domini.*

His voice grew softer and softer, farther and farther away, and then we slept.[1]

The almost purely Latin words "dictum," "domini," "Partem" ("Partum" in the Wilson version), "quantum," and "centum" suggest a relationship to the Roman Catholic liturgy. Father Francis J. Murphy, of the Chapel of St. Thomas More, Chapel Hill, whom I asked about these

---

[1]Reprinted by permission of the Editors of the *Saturday Evening Post* and of Mrs. Eleanor Wilson McAdoo of Santa Barbara, California.

words, suggests that "Partem quantum" may be a corruption and transposition of "Quantum possem" in the Absolution. On the point of Roman Catholic influence so far as her version is concerned, Mrs. Lanphere says that her father's family had no Catholic connections. On the contrary, it was Scots-Irish Presbyterian, as was Woodrow Wilson's family.

If "Perry Merry Dictum Domini" is in part a parody of the Roman liturgy, it would not have had to come from a Catholic *milieu* or a Protestant satire on the liturgy within the last four hundred years. Many of the old Child ballads have a pre-Reformation reference and apparently come from a time when the great majority of British people were no longer Roman Catholic but continued to use the language of the Mother Church. Phrases from the Roman liturgy were, as most educated people realize, taken over into *The Book of Common Prayer*. They have found their way into the folklore of people to whom the Catholic liturgy is alien, as in a line from a counting-out rhyme I learned in Mississippi—"Virgin Mary, hail 'em, scale 'em."

The Oxford Dictionary of Nursery Rhymes includes a full version of the lullaby, extensive historical notes, and a plate from a photograph of a fifteenth-century English song which includes many of its principal features. The first stanza runs:

> I have four sisters beyond the sea,
>   Perrie, Merrie, Dixie, Dominie;
> And they each sent a present to me,
>   Petrum, Partrum, Paradisi, Temporie,
>   Perrie, Merrie, Dixie, Domini.

The presents are the same as those in the Wilson and Lanphere versions—chicken, cherry, book, and blanket (coat in Lanphere), and the order is the same as that of the Wilson. The order in the Lanphere is coat, book, cherry, chicken. *The Oxford Dictionary* version has a question, "How can there be?" for each object, and concludes:

> When the chicken's in the egg-shell there is no bone,
> *Refrain.*
> When the cherry's in the bud, there is no stone,
> *Refrain.*
>
> When the book's in the press, no man it can read,
> *Refrain.*
> When the blanket's in the fleece there is no thread,
> *Refrain.*

The editors remark, "This has been thought of as a children's song for anyway 150 years," and cite reports of the occurrence of it in England, where it was first reported in 1866 by a correspondent to *Notes and Queries* who remembered "hearing it many years previously." They sum up with the statement: "The survival of the song is remarkable. For 500 years it has been carried in the wallet of popular memory, and for four of these centuries successfully evaded exposure on the printed page."

Finally, they print from "a small manuscript collection of songs and carols made in the first half of the fifteenth century" a poem beginning with almost the same couplet as that of their nineteenth-century text and containing two of the riddles and answers—cherry and dove (for chicken). They observe that "this may have been old when written down"—500 years ago!

Though it gives American versions and variants of many nursery rhymes, *The Oxford Dictionary of Nursery Rhymes* does not give any American texts of this lullaby or cite any instances of its occurrence in America.

A version of "Peri Meri Dictum Domini" has come to me from one of my colleagues, Professor O. B. Hardison. He said that he has known the song for some time, that he learned it from a young woman in Connecticut who did not tell him her source, and that, like Woodrow Wilson, he was accustomed to sing it to his five young daughters. Professor Hardison sang his version for tape recording, and Professor Daniel W. Patterson, another colleague, noted the tune and the words for me as follows:

I HAD FOUR BROTH-ERS ALL O-VER THE SEA

PER-RY MER-RY DI-XI DO-MI-NI EACH OF THEM BROUGHT A

PRES-ENT TO ME PAN-TRUM TAN-TRUM PAR-A-DISE QUAR-TUM

PER-RY MER-RY DI-XI DO-MI-NI.

PERRY MERRY DICTUM DOMINI

I had four brothers all over the sea,
   Perry merry dixi domini;
Each of them brought a present to me,
   Pantrum tantrum paradise quartum,
   Perry merry dixi domini.

First was a ring without no end,
   Perry merry dixi domini;
Second was a book that no man's read,
   Pantrum tantrum paradise quartum,
   Perry merry dixi domini.

Third was a cherry without no stone,
　Perry merry dixi domini;
Fourth was a chicken without no bone,
　Pantrum tantrum paradise quartum,
　Perry merry dixi domini.

How can there be a ring without no end?
How can there be a book that no man's read?

How can there be a cherry without no stone?
How can there be a chicken without no bone?

A ring when it's rolling it has no end;
A book in the press, that no man's read;

A cherry when it's blooming it has no stone;
A chicken when it's pipping it has no bone.

Other American versions of "Peri Meri Dictum Domini" seem to be scarce. The song is not cited in *An Analytical Index to the Journal of American Folklore.* However, there are two published American versions.

The first is given by Mary O. Eddy in her *Ballads and Songs from Ohio* as a version of "Captain Wedderburn's Courtship," which it seems clearly not to be, and with footnote references, mostly to the so-called "Riddle Song" which many scholars apparently regard as derived from the Child ballad. This version, with music and text, under the title "Perry Merry Dictum Domini," is given as from Miss Lena Smith, Medina, Ohio, procured by Miss Helen Hobart. It varies slightly in the "Latin" refrain and has the cherry, chicken, blanket, and book riddles, with answers.

The other published American version is that by John Jacob Niles in *Schirmer's American Folk-Song Series, Set 17: More Songs of the Hill-Folk,* etc. This, notes the book, was "Recorded at Berea, Kentucky, from the singing of Miss Cora L. Swift, who lives in Oberlin, Ohio. Miss Swift learned the song from Miss Phoebe M. Hayes, whose parents came from Massachusetts (where their ancestors landed in 1636) by way of Mendham, N. Y." Mr. Niles gives no comparative notes and cites none.

The words of the Niles version, besides in the spelling of the refrain portion given in the title, differ from the words in the Lanphere and Eddy versions in a few particulars: "Pantrum quartrum paradise Stantrum" in the rest of the refrain; "three cousins" for "four brothers"; "Three or four presents sent they me" for "They each brought a present unto me"; "a bird without a bone" (this riddle being first) for "chicken"; "book that no man's read" (third riddle); "blanket without a thread," as in the Wilson version, for "coat without a thread"; and differences in the answers corresponding to differences in the objects named. The music of this version, with piano accompaniment, seems to differ considerably from the version of Mrs. Lanphere.

It appears, then, that Mrs. Lanphere's "Perry Merry Dictum Domini" has an attested pedigree of oral tradition as long as, or longer than, the English published version. Compare the *Notes & Queries* record and text of 1866, the given date of transmission modified by the vague phrase "many years previously," with the precise fact of Dr. Downing's birth date, 1856, and Mrs. Lanphere's statement that her father had learned the song from his father in early childhood and that it had then been long in the family, first in Maryland, then in Virginia. Its pedigree is more definite and perhaps older than that of the other American versions. Woodrow Wilson was born in 1856, too, but his daughter does not state when and from whom he learned his version. Mrs. Lanphere's version is more exactly dated and related to family history than are Woodrow Wilson's, Miss Eddy's, Mr. Niles's, or Professor Hardison's.

A highly important advantage, shared by Mrs. Lanphere's version with Miss Eddy's, Mr. Niles's, and Professor Hardison's, is that it has the music. *The Oxford Dictionary of Nursery Rhymes* says nothing about a tune for its version. Mrs. Eleanor Wilson McAdoo, if she remembered it (as quite probably she did, because she remembered the words, and the tune is so simple), unfortunately did not include the tune with Woodrow Wilson's version as reported in the *Post*. In a letter to me, dated April 3, 1961, she stated that the tune of Mrs. Lanphere's version, sent to her, and sung by Mr. James Pirrie, a musician friend in Santa Barbara, California, is recognizably the same as her father's. Other than the versions cited here, I have not been able to find published notices or texts of the song.

In one version or another, with little license or benefit of print, and slight notice of scholars, "Perry Merry Dictum Domini" has survived the drums and tramplings and cannonades and destructions of many wars, conquests, and revolutions. It has held its own from the time of King Henry the Sixth, when Joan of Arc was burned at the stake, down to the present, when rocket ships are being sent into outer space.

Why has "Perry Merry Dictum Domini" survived, and without the aid of a grant from some foundation, agency, or rich individual to record the words and notes in microfilm, photostat, script, or type?

Perhaps it is because "Perry Merry Dictum Domini" has participated in the immortal spirit of childhood, living on the lips of those who love and cherish children: the obscure young professor Woodrow Wilson, in the nursery of a Princeton faculty house, romping on the floor with his little girls, making funny faces, and singing away their fears and loneliness with "Peri Meri Dictum Domini"; the young Dr. Downing, graduate of Rush Medical College, Chicago, giving up a rich income from fashionable city patients to treat the ills and wounds and deliver the babies of Swedish, German, Polish, Bohemian, and American pioneer peasants and farmers on the prairies of Nebraska, and lulling his babies to sleep and diverting the tedium of long horse-and-buggy drives to and from farmhouses, for his little girl; Professor Hardison singing it to his five children in Chapel Hill, North Carolina.

Will "Perry Merry Dictum Domini" abide still in an atomic age? Is it destined to be like "Oranges and lemons, say the bells of St. Clement's," about which George Orwell said in his *1984,* "The little nursery rhyme has become the symbol of a human and beautiful past"? Or will the chopper come to cut off its head?

If the goblins get it and all the rest, will men and women wish to live longer in a world which will not care for and perpetuate such tremendous trifles?

LECTURE

TWO

Glimpses of History in Folksongs of the South

THE SEVENTEENTH-CENTURY ANTIQUARY JOHN AUBREY ONCE remarked that "before women were readers, the history of England was handed down from mother to daughter. . . . So my nurse had the history from the Conquest down to Carolus I in ballad." Many of the historical ballads known to seventeenth-century mothers and nurses have been preserved in such great collections as the Roxburghe, the Bagford, and the Pepys. Readers of Francis J. Child's *The English and Scottish Popular Ballads* will recall the chronicle type, of which "The Battle of Otterburn," "The Hunting of the Cheviot," and "King Henry Fifth's Conquest of France" are famous examples. Of the 305 Child ballads, around ten per cent, some of these the best in the collection, treat historical events.

In America, historical ballads and the oral tradition that preserved them were retained by our colonial ancestors. Students of American literature are familiar with Cotton Mather's complaint about the popularity of secular ballads in early New England and with a few pieces treating such Virginia episodes as Bacon's Rebellion. We know, too, that the American Revolution was fought with ballads as well as bullets, as in "The Battle of the Kegs" and "Yankee Doodle." The tradition of celebrating and commemorating historical events in song has persisted. In practically every collection of American folksongs there is a varying number devoted to events, movements, and causes of more than local interest, thus reflecting what we call history.

A brief survey of typical collections from the South will indicate the ratio of historical pieces. One of the earliest and most representative, J. H. Cox's *Folksongs of the South,* with 185 ballads and songs, has 24 historical pieces. On the other hand, Josiah H. Combs's *Folksongs du Midi des Etats Unis,* gathered from much of the same area as Cox's, has but three historical songs in 61. A. P. Hudson's *Folksongs of Mississippi* has 13 out of 157; M. E. Henry's *Folksongs from the Southern Highlands,* six out of 180; Alton C. Morris's *Folksongs of Florida,* 17 out of 243. It is one of the distinctions of Dr. Morris's collection that it contains one of the very few Child ballads known in America that were based on British history—"Lord Derwentwater" (Child No. 208), connected with the rising in 1715 in the North of England in behalf of the Pretender. Arthur Kyle Davis's *Folk-Songs of Virginia, a Descriptive Index and Classification* lists 32 historical songs.

The largest number of historical folksongs occurring in any single American collection known to me is to be found in *The Frank C. Brown Collection of North Carolina Folklore.* As one of the two editors of the ballads and songs in the *Collection,* I count 68 historical folksongs in the 989 pieces selected by the editors for publication. Since many of these 68 occur also in other collections, state, regional, and national, I make these the basis from which to survey, with occasional notice of other collections, the historical folksongs in the South.

— As might be expected, most of the historical songs have to do with wars. Of these, "Boney's Defeat" and "The Isle of St. Helena," both treating Napoleon's downfall and exile, and "Waterloo" and "The Drummer Boy of Waterloo" are the most common. There is, too, "Flora MacDonald's Lament," in the *Brown Collection,* a sentimental piece connected with the Scottish heroine's rescue of Prince Charles Edward Stuart from the hands of his enemies after the Battle of Culloden, in 1746. The song was preserved by descendants of the Tory Highlanders who were defeated at the Widow Moore's Creek, in 1776.

— As is true of American folksong collections in general, the Southern collections have few pieces going back to Colonial times. The *Brown Collection,* however, has a unique group of songs relating to the Regulator troubles of 1765-1771. Originally composed by a schoolteacher in Randolph County, in derision of extortionate and dishonest King's officers at Hillsboro, these songs were sung at Regulator rallies all over the frontier area affected by the resistance movement that ended at the Battle of Alamance and with the hanging of six Regulators, in 1771. One of the songs, a ballad, and the traditional account accompanying it tell how the Regulators rode to Hillsboro, the provincial capital, to rescue two of their friends from jail; how Colonel Fanning, clerk of the court there, and one of the chief extortioners, met them at the Eno River boundary of the town, told them that their friends had been released, and begged them to disperse; how, to enforce his plea, the Colonel waded the river with a bottle of wine in one hand and a bottle of rum in the other; and how the leader of the Regulators, an old Scotsman, put the Colonel in his place. By a rare stroke of luck, this song and two others were in 1819 copied by the clerk of

the Supreme Court at Hillsboro into court records, from
the recitation of an old-timer who remembered the Regulator troubles and the songs. These songs of course passed
out of oral tradition many years ago. Not so "Brave
Wolfe," reported by Combs from West Virginia, which
was remembered as late as 1925. Its nineteen stanzas describe the Battle of Quebec, in which Generals Wolfe
and Montcalm were killed.

The American Revolution is somewhat better recalled.
Cox's "Revolutionary Tea," traditional in West Virginia,
tells how "an old lady who lived over the sea/Called on
her daughters to pay her a tax/Of threepence a pound on
tea," and how "the bouncing girl poured out every
pound." The same ballad is found in Morris's Florida
collection. Another in the Morris collection, "Yankee
Doodle," differing from the familiar song of that name,
explains how the tea tax started the Revolution. A third
Florida song relates how George Washington made the
British invaders "shudder from the happy land of Canaan."
The Frank C. Brown Collection contains four songs belonging to the period. "The Rolling Neuse" describes how,
"when Greene's horn blew a long, loud blast," a young
man felt those conflicting emotions of love for country
and love for his Nancy that young men have felt since
wars began. "The Jolly Soldier" is an old song refurbished
"for the honor of George Washington." "Paul Jones,"
sung in the North Carolina coast country, is a spirited
account of the victory won by the *Bonhomme Richard*
off the coast of England in 1778. Historical context justifies
mention again of "Flora MacDonald's Lament," a love
song pure and simple, that connects, on the one hand,
with the old Jacobite sentiment of the Highland Scots
and, on the other, with the story of a heroic woman who
sojourned briefly in North Carolina, encouraging her men-

folk to participate in an abortive Tory rising, and left behind her a shining and tragic legend.

In North Carolina, too, perhaps by reason of its long maritime history, has been well preserved the most famous sea ballad of the Revolution. "Paul Jones," represented by two versions in *The Brown Collection,* is an account of the victory won off Flamborough Head, Yorkshire, September 21, 1778, by Commodore Paul Jones, with the *Bonhomme Richard* and the *Pallas,* from the British ships *Serapis* and *Countess of Scarborough.* John Paul Jones lived for a while in Wilmington, North Carolina. The following is the version contributed by P. D. Midgett, Jr., from Wanchese, June 5, 1920:

A forty-gun frigate from Baltimore came,
Her guns mounted forty, and *Richard* by name,
Went cruising the channel of old England,
With a noble commander, Paul Jones was the man.

We had not sailed long before we did spy
A large forty-four and a twenty close by,
All these warlike vessels full laden with store;
Our captain pursued them on the bold York shore.

At the hour of twelve Pierce came alongside
With a large speaking trumpet: "Whence came you?" he
    cried.
"Quick give me an answer, I've hailed you before.
Or at this moment a broadside I'll pour."

We fought them five glasses, five glasses so hot,
Till sixty bright seamen lay dead on the spot,
Full seventy wounded lay bleeding in gore.
How fierce our loud cannons on the *Richard* did roar.

Our gunner got frightened, to Paul Jones he came.
"Our ship she is sinking, likewise in a flame."
Paul Jones he smiled in the height of his pride,
Saying, "This day I'll conquer or sink alongside."

Here's health to those widows who shortly must weep,
For the loss of their husbands who sunk in the deep.
Here's a health to those young girls who shortly must
   mourn
For the loss of their sweethearts that's **overboard** thrown.

Here's a health to Paul Jones with sword in hand . . .
He was foremost in action, in giving command.
Here's a health to Paul Jones and all his crew . . .
If we hadn't a French Captain, boys, what could we do!

This is probably the source of a version from C. K.
(Pink) Tillett of Wanchese, obtained by Frank Warner
of Farringdale, New York, and recorded for me by Mr.
Warner on September 9, 1961. Mr. Warner's handling of
the Outer Banks dialect is a notable feature of this recording, as it is of all his fine folksong albums.

From the War of 1812 have come down several battle
pieces. The best of these are "James Bird," in *The Frank
C. Brown Collection,* and several others. After fighting
bravely in the Battle of Lake Erie, James Bird deserted.
He was courtmartialed and shot. Soon afterwards Charles
Miner composed a ballad on Bird's fate and published it
in a Pennsylvania newspaper. Thence it passed into oral
tradition. One ballad scholar asks, "Has this country pro-
duced any historical ballad that has passed into tradition,
which is more interesting than this?" The vigorous and
picturesque "Hunters of Kentucky," celebrating Andrew
Jackson's victory at New Orleans and helping to give cur-
rency to the phrase "half horse, half alligator," has been
reported from Tennessee.

Except in the old playparty song "Going to the Mexican
War," present in most Southern collections, the Mexican
War left few traces in folksong.

The American Civil War, however, bequeathed a large
number that survived well into the present century. In the

leaflet accompanying Frank Warner's album *Songs of the Civil War,* the editor remarks:

"The Civil War was a singing war, and the songs of that time . . . many of them sad and sentimental, some with a tough, battle-seasoned humor . . . tell us much that the history books may leave out, and let us share the moods of the soldiers in a way that the history books cannot do. In his book *The Life of Billy Yank,* Bell Irvin Wiley tells how the troops in the 1860's went to war with songs on their lips: 'They sang on the march, in the trenches, on fatigue, in the guardhouse, on the battlefield, and especially in bivouac. The urge to sing was so irrepressible that men on outpost duty sometimes had to be reprimanded for lifting their voices and giving away their positions.'

"Men sang alone and they sang together. A banjo or a fiddle was often a part of a soldier's personal equipment. Soldiers brought songs from home; they swapped songs with each other and with soldiers on the other side; they learned songs in the homes of people they visited wherever they were stationed; they bought sheet music whenever possible. Songs gave the men hope and comfort and courage; on a number of occasions they turned the tide of battle. Songs are an integral part of the Civil War story."[1]

The Frank C. Brown Collection alone has over thirty Civil War songs, many of them in common with other Southern collections. Among these, "The *Cumberland,*" relating a famous exploit of the Confederate ironclad *Virginia,* is one of the liveliest. Both it and "The Dying Fifer," originally broadsides, of which I found copies in the Harvard Library, were remembered on the North Carolina coast. "The Battle of Shiloh," "The Drummer Boy of Shiloh," and "Brother Green" dwell impartially

---

1. Frank Warner, *Songs of the Civil War,* Prestige Records, Inc., 203 So. Washington Ave., Bergenfield, N. J.

on the sadness of death and severed family ties. "The Good Old Rebel," which the Prince of Wales (afterwards Edward VIII) liked for its "cuss words," has its counterpart in "The Veteran's Song." The following titles will indicate the range of pieces related to specific battles: "The Vicksburg Soldier," "The Battle of Mill Springs," and "The Battle of Fredericksburg."

Many of the songs, like "Root Hog or Die" and "The Southern Wagon," are devoted to issues of the conflict. In North Carolina variants about him, John Brown's body suffers a sea change. "The Bonnie Blue Flag" takes on new stanzas as additional states secede.

Some of the songs suggest the stresses and strains of war. In "The Homespun Dress" speaks the clear, resolute voice of the women of the South. The fighting spirit of "Never Mind Your Knapsack" is contradicted by "The Bushwacker's Song" and "Deserter's Song." The last-named reads:

> I'd ruther be on the Grandfather Mountain
> A-taking the snow and rain
> Than to be in Castle Thunder
> A-wearin' the ball and chain.

It illustrates ways in which history is sometimes obscurely embedded in a song. Grandfather Mountain is easily identified as a peak near Boone. But what is Castle Thunder? I spent hours in vain trying to find out. The answer came unexpectedly in Ben Ames Williams's *House Divided* and was confirmed by the Questions and Answers file of the *Richmond Times-Dispatch*. Castle Thunder was a provost-prison in Richmond during the Civil War. In "Come Rain" and "Sorghum Molasses," the seasoned old campaigner turned forager sings in the dryly, whimsically humorous nostalgia of one who remembers the fleshpots of peace. An authentic concoction of cornbread, sorghum

molasses, and goobers, mixed by Tar Heel and Cracker
wit, and consumed in the remembered smile of a blue-eyed
Georgia girl, "Sorghum Molasses," from *The Frank C.
Brown Collection,* deserves to be quoted:

>A soldier was settin' by the road one day,
>And he was a-lookin' very gay.
>By his side he had some meal
>That he'd just stolen from an old Tar Heel.
>Bye and bye.

>*Chorus:*
>I'm a-goin' to marry before I die,
>Bye and bye, bye and bye,
>Marry the girl with the bright blue eyes.
>The Georgia girl there's none surpasses;
>They are sweeter far than sorghum molasses.
>Bye and bye.

>He made a fire to bake his bread,
>And when it was done he laughed and said,
>"In all the world there's none surpasses
>Good cornbread and sorghum molasses."
>Bye and bye.

>In a canteen by his side
>That he was tryin' hard to hide
>From the pryin' eyes of all by-passers
>He had a quart of sorghum molasses.
>Bye and bye.

>As I went up Atlanta street
>A Tar Heel girl I chanced to meet.
>Says to me, "Are you a traveler?"
>"Yes, by ginger, I'm a goober grabbler."
>Bye and bye.

>There's Alabama, everybody sees,
>Tennessee, or what you please,
>South Carolina, tar and rosum,
>Good old Georgia, goobers and sorghum.
>Bye and bye.

— Consistent with the Napoleonic maxim that an army travels on its belly, many of the most heart-felt and genuine folksongs have to do with the soldier's preoccupation with grub. This was especially true of the Confederate soldier, whose service of supply was chronically haphazard. The closely related needs for drink, shelter, and women also found their expression in wryly doleful songs. I quote several of these. The first two run the gamut of themes; the others specialize on grub.

CIVIL WAR SONG

You good folks don't scarcely know
What we poor soldiers undergo
When called upon to take up arms
To defend our country from all harms.

At break of day the morning dawn
Is regulated by the fife and drum,
To break the soldier's sweet repose.
He rises up, puts on his clothes.

As for the grog, we have enough,
Although our beef is lean and tough.
But for this we won't complain,
For we hope to draw good beef again.

If you want to know who composed this song,
I'll tell you now; it won't be long.
It was composed by A. T. Hyte,
While walking post one cold winter night.

A HUNGRY CONFEDERATE SONG

The streets are all lonely and drear, love,
And all because you are not here, love.
If you were, you would shed a sad tear, love,
    And open your cupboard to me.

My feet are all wet with the dew, love;
There's nothing so good as hot stew, love;
Oh, get up and make some, pray do, love,
    And open your cupboard to me.

Get out of your soft feather bed, love,
And make me a pone of cornbread, love,
I'm suffering now to be fed, love,
    And open your cupboard to me.

I'LL EAT WHEN I'M HUNGRY

I'll eat when I'm hungry,
    I'll drink when I'm dry.
If the Yankees don't get me
    I'll live till I die.

"Goober Peas" does not often appear in the folksong anthologies, but it has achieved popularity through the singing of Burl Ives and other present-day minstrels, and it sounds authentic enough. Its insulting remark about the Georgia militia is the sort of touch that gives folksongs verve and memorableness.

GOOBER PEAS

Peas, peas, peas, peas! Goodness,
How delicious eating goober peas!

Sitting by the roadside on a summer's day,
Chatting with my messmates, passing time away,
Lying in the shadow underneath the trees,
Goodness, how delicious, eating goober peas!
    Peas, peas, etc.

When a horseman passes, soldiers have a rule
To cry out at their loudest, "Hey, mister, here's your
    mule!"
But another pleasure enchantinger than these
Is wearing out your grinders eating goober peas.
    Peas, peas, etc.

Just before the battle the general hears a row.
He says, "The Yanks are coming, I hear their rifles now."
He turned around in wonder, and what do you think he
    sees?
The Georgia militia cracking goober peas.
    Peas, peas, peas, peas,
        The Georgia militia cracking goober peas,

I think my song has lasted almost long enough.
The subject's interesting, but the rimes are mighty rough.
I wish this war was over and free from rags and fleas,
To kiss our wives and sweethearts and gobble goober peas.

> Peas, peas, peas, peas. Goodness,
> How delicious eating goober peas![2]

Perhaps the classic epilogue upon the War Between the States started out as an art poem, without the author's dreaming that it would be a folksong.

"The Good Old Rebel" was composed originally by Innes Randolph, a Baltimore lawyer, who had been on Jeb Stuart's staff, and during Reconstruction became fed up on the policy the North was pursuing toward the conquered South. The poem became so popular that it was set to music and was soon on its way to being a folksong by acceptance. Many ex-Confederate soldiers who sang it laid claim to its authorship. But there is no doubt about its authorship. It is included in *Poems by Innes Randolph*. The following is a folk version of it from Mississippi.

I served with old Bob Lee three years about,
Got wounded in four places and starved at Point Lookout.
I caught the rheumatism campin' in the snow.
I killed a sight o' Yankees, and wish I'd killed som mo'.

Chorus:

For I'm a good old rebel, that's what I am,
And for the Land o' Freedom I don't care a damn.
I'm glad I fought against her; I only wish we'd won.
And I don't ask no pardons for anything I've done.

---

2. Frank Warner's version, recorded in *Songs of the Civil War*, Prestige International Record 13012, Prestige Records, Inc., 203 So. Washington Ave., Bergenfield, N. J. There is a version consisting of one stanza and the chorus in Byron Arnold's *Folksongs of Alabama* (University, Alabama: University of Alabama Press, 1950), p. 100.

I hate the Constitution, the Great Republic too;
I hate the mighty eagle and the uniform of blue.
I hate the Glorious Banner and all their flags and fuss;
Them lyin', thievin' Yankees, I hate 'em wuss and wuss.

I won't be reconstructed, I'm better now than them;
For those dirty carpetbaggers I don't give a damn.
So I'm off to the Border as soon as I can go;
I'll git me a gun and leave for Mexico.

Later wars left a small detritus of traditional folksong. One group views the Spanish-American War, with attempted heroics in "Manila Bay," with pathos in two pieces about the battleship *Maine,* and with cynicism in "That Bloody War." The last-named was adapted to World War I, maintaining its "songs-that-mother-never-taught me" tone. And the ballad muse brings her work almost up to date in "Just Remember Pearl Harbor," a Negro recital of atrocities that precipitated our country into World War II. Perhaps all the war songs of all the ages, of this country and of all countries, find laconic utterance of the simple annals of the GI in "Soldier's Epitaph," from World War I:

Born in North Carolina,
Raised in Tennessee,
Worked like hell in Georgia,
Died in Germanee.

Non-military events and movements are recalled by smaller groups of songs. Faint echoes of party strife persist in old campaign songs. The "ballad-deafened" contest of 1840, between General William Henry Harrison ("Old Tippecanoe") and President Martin Van Buren, is represented by "Tippecanoe." In another, Henry Clay is satirized to the tune of "Old Dan Tucker":

Henry Clay, he climbed a tree
And stuck his bill in for to see.
The lizards caught him by the snout,
And he hollered for the coons to pull him out.

Chorus:
Get out the way, roll on lucky;
Clear the track for old Kentucky.

Henry Clay came riding a jack;
He rode on his belly to save his back.
Oh, riding a goat and leading a sheep,
And he won't get back till the middle of the week.

Only reference to newspapers and detailed political histories of the 1870's would connect "Does Your Mother Know You're Out" with Horace Greeley's campaign for the presidency in 1872. "Joe Bowers" and "The Dying Californian" have their setting in the Gold Rush of 1849. The assassination of President James A. Garfield is preserved in folk memory by the dolorous "Charles Guiteau."— Maritime disasters are commemorated in such ballads as "Wreck of the *Huron*," "Wreck of the *Lady Elgin*," and "The *Titanic*," all of which succeed in transmitting a shock of national or even world-wide magnitude. As a final instance, "The *Shenandoah*," about the wreck of a famous dirigible, may be cited to show how the ballad muse becomes air-minded. The spirited, journalistic ballad "Roger Young," about the heroic and self-sacrificing death of an American soldier in the Pacific theater of World War II, has become almost traditional.

A comparison of these American historical folksongs with their British analogues would show much to be wished for in our own products, and yet it would reveal much in them that we value. It seems that the poetic excellence of folksongs celebrating events is inversely proportional to the importance of events. Bigger battles in

America have not made better ballads. Nothing in native American heroic balladry equals the nervous energy, the chivalric spirit, and the heroic tone of "Otterburn" or "Chevy Chase." There is no American rival for the stanza describing Montgomery's death:

> The dynt it was both sad and sar
>   that he of Monggomberry sete;
> The swane-fethars that his arrow bar
>   with his hart-blood the ware wete.

And yet the native American pieces exhibit humor and sentiment, a sense of the comedy and the sadness of war, and an awareness of the share of the common man in the making of history—qualities more precious, perhaps, in popular American esteem than the heroic traits of the older British balladry. In their way these more prosaic qualities help keep the past alive.

LECTURE

THREE

Folksongs in American Poetry and Fiction

FOLKSONGS IN POETRY

AT CAIRO, ILLINOIS, THE OHIO JOINS THE MISSISSIPPI. IT IS said that for some miles below the junction point, one can distinguish by its clear stream the Ohio from the muddy Father of Waters. Yet who could speak accurately of the "impact" of the Ohio on the Mississippi? They are both basically water, with various organic and inorganic matter in solution or afloat. So with folklore and poetry. They are both creations of the human fantasy or imagination operating upon the material of human experiences. In primitive ages they are indistinguishable, so that your *Iliad* and *Odyssey*, your *Beowulf* and *Kalevala* are at the same time your magazines of folklore and your supreme poems. It is only when imagination grows conscious of itself and of its materials, aims, and methods that folklore in a substantial sense becomes art poetry. So it falls to me to try to show the point at which American poetry grows conscious of itself as American and of its subjects, its aims, and its art as American, and to survey some of the results.

I cannot fix that point precisely in time-space. It is approximately established, however, in Robert Frost's "The Gift Outright." We came to this land as British, Irish, French, German, Scandinavian, Spanish, African, et cetera, bearing with us the folksongs, folktales, legends, myths, proverbs, riddles, games, customs, and beliefs of our homelands. Here we found another race and another folklore, both alien and incomprehensible, and at first both horrendous and unassimilable. For a hundred years "we were England's, still colonials," singing our babies to sleep with "Froggie Went a-Courting" and "Old Bangum," making love with "Lord Randal" and "Bonny Barbara Allan's Cruelty," twitting our women with the proverb of the leaky roof and the scolding wife, celebrating our heroes with ballads about Robin Hood, entertaining the chimney corner with the Wives of St. Ives. And we still do, for that matter. But as the shores of the old homelands receded in distance and time, we grew restless and uneasy—

> Possessing what we still were unpossessed by,
> Possessed by what we now no more possessed.

And our people, long before the poets, were possessed by this land, and possessed it. We unconsciously adapted the old folklore to the new scene. The English and Scottish ballads "have become as American as anything not Red Indian can be."

> Songs of my people, the cuckoo's voice
>   Dies out, faint and forlorn,
> And louder caws the garden thief
>   That pecks the farmer's corn.
> The raven's now an old black crow;
>   He spies no knight new-slain—
> Merely the carcass of a horse
>   A-lying in the lane.

We learned to paddle our own canoe. Also, we observed that "The bigger they are, the harder they fall." And often, too often perhaps, we went

> All the way to Arkansaw
> To eat cornbread and possum jaw.

From the beginning of American literature until the early years of the Romantic Period, connections between art poetry and folklore were incidental and more or less consistent with British precedent.[1] Until well into the nineteenth century broadside and newspaper ballads were staple reading provender. Franklin and, later, Bryant and Cooper wrote ballads for newspapers and itinerant singers and peddlers. Royall Tyler's "Ode Composed for the Fourth of July" (1786) gives a gusty list of folk customs, including game songs and dances. Freneau occasionally used folksong patterns, as in the come-all-ye "Barney's Invitation" and "The Battle of Stonington." His "The Indian Student" and "The Indian Burying Ground" show sympathetic interest in Indian character, custom, and belief. Joel Barlow's "The Hasty Pudding" is a mock-heroic but savory treatment of the folklore of native food—Polanta, Polante, mush, Suppawn, and Hasty Pudding. Bryant's "The Little People of the Snow" is a tedious attempt to tell a fairy tale in blank verse. His "Monument Mountain" (1824) more successfully treats a local legend. It is one of the earliest poetic handlings of the lover's-leap story, with Indian characters and setting. Bryant's "The Prairies" contains an extensive account of the mysterious Mound-Builders. His "Song of Marion's Men" (1831), a ballad — celebrating the exploits of the South Carolina Swamp Fox _

---

1. In this and several following paragraphs, I am indebted to the Macmillan Company for permission to make considerable use of my article "Folklore" in *Literary History of the United States,* ed. Robert Spiller, Willard Thorp, *et al.,* 3 vols. (New York: The Macmillan Company, 1948), 715-16, 727.

and his band, had the ironical fate of becoming a favorite
song around Confederate campfires during the Civil War.
"The Adventures of the Green Mountain Boys" treats
heroic material belonging to New England. Though Poe's
fiction utilizes American folklore to some extent, his
poetry owes little to folklore except the form and technique of the Romantic ballad as in "The Raven" and
"Annabel Lee."

In Longfellow and Whittier treatment of American
folklore goes somewhat beyond the conventions established by British Romantics. In them we begin to see the
workings of the yeast which animates Emerson's "Phi Beta
Kappa Address."

Whittier's "Snowbound" makes rich allusive use of folklore in painting the humble life of a New England family.
Childish fancy

> Whispered the old rhyme, *Under the Tree*
> *When fire outdoors burns merrily,*
> *There the witches are making tea.*
>
> . . . .
>
> We sped the time in stories old,
> Wrought puzzles out, and riddles told.

In a later couplet with the same rhymes he recalls "tales
of witchcraft." The father remembers the violin "which
did the village dancers sway" in the French towns. The
mother

> Told how the Indian bands came down
> At midnight on Cocheeco town,
>
> . . . .
>
> Recalling in her fitting phrase,
>   So rich and picturesque and free
>   (The common unrhymed poetry
> Of simple life and country ways),
> The story of her early days.
>
> . . . .
>
> We stole with her a frightened look
> At the grey wizard's conjuring-book.

The schoolmaster is a well-drawn folk character, versed in the rustic party games, skilled on the merry violin and adept at retelling the "classic legends rare and old" which he had learned in Dartmouth's college halls, in "mirth provoking version." When time dragged, the family re-read the Almanac and conned the village paper for "jest, anecdote, and love-lorn tale." Whittier's "Songs of Slaves in the Desert" suggests the old spirituals, especially in the refrain, "Where are we going, Rubee?" "The Wreck of Rivermouth" is based on the legend of a seventeenth-century witch who cast a spell on a fishing boat, and upon her death was buried with a stake through her body. "Telling the Bees" treats "a remarkable custom brought from the Old Country, formerly prevalent in the rural districts of New England." "The Huskers" is a pleasing picture of a characteristically American rural festival, with its "husky ballad" sung by the schoolmaster. The familiar "Maud Muller" is an idyllic ballad. Whittier's most successful short efforts are his ballads treating American historical or traditional themes. "Brown of Ossawatomie," in fourteeners, is a worthy forerunner of fine poems by Carl Sandburg and Stephen Vincent Benét. "Barbara Frietchie" is known to most schoolboys as a spirited treatment of an incident in the Confederate invasion of the North. Whittier's finest achievement in the ballad is "Skipper Ireson's Ride," with its swift and violent action and its tarry and salty folk speech.

Longfellow is the most systematic exploiter of American folklore. Three of his major poems would alone offer material for a substantial study. *Evangeline,* besides utilizing much historical material, owes a great deal to legend and other types of folklore. Not content with the main traditional outlines of his story, he carefully worked up the Arcadian folk beliefs. The old notary of Grand Pré was beloved of the children,

For he told them tales of the Loup-Garou in the forest,
And of the goblin that came in the night to water the horses
And of the white letiche, the ghost of the child who un-
    christened
Died, and was doomed to haunt the unseen chambers of
    children;
And how on Christmas eve the oxen talked in the stable,
And how the fever was cured by a spider shut up in a nutshell,
And of the marvelous powers of four-leaved clover and horse-
    shoes,
And whatsoever was writ in the lore of the village.

In the Ozark Country Evangeline and Basil listened to
the Shawnee woman's "tale of the fair Lilinau who was
wooed by a phantom," until she felt "That, like the Indian
maid, she too, was pursuing a phantom." *Hiawatha* (1855),
based on Henry R. Schoolcraft's monumental studies of
the American Indians, is the earliest successful effort at
an American epic. Taking his verse form from the Finnish
epic, *The Kalevala,* Longfellow tried to make *Hiawatha*
"This Indian Edda—if I may so call it." The measure of
his success is suggested by Stith Thompson's remark that
"it is through *Hiawatha* that most Americans even now
learn what little they know about the American Indian
story."[2] *The Courtship of Miles Standish* (1857-58) was
based on traditions well known before Longfellow took up
the story. These three long poems, drawing in part from
folkloristic sources, in turn "did something to stay if not
to satisfy America's hunger for a past, a legendry, a body
of myth of her own."[3]

Such were the origins and such the effects of Longfellow's *Tales of a Wayside Inn* and his other short poems.
If his subjects were not already folklore, he sought to
make them such, in the manner of eighteenth-century

2. "The Indian Heritage," *Literary History of the United States,*
II, 694.

3. Odell Shepard, "The New England Triumvirate," *ibid.,* 593.

English Romantics, who, if they did not have medieval ruins on their estates, carefully constructed ruins, or the University of Chicago, which is alleged to have smoked and dusted its brand-new Gothic building to give it the proper patina. "Thus, in writing 'The Wreck of the Hesperus,' less than two weeks after the incident it describes and within fifty miles of its scene, he made it sound as much as possible like a medieval popular ballad." A recent critic has complained that "The scenes of his three long narrative poems with an ostensible American setting might almost have been laid in Arcadia, so devoid they are of sharp factual detail and contemporary reference."[4] In "The Village Blacksmith," "The Building of the Ship," and "The Shoemakers" Longfellow attempts a gentlemanly treatment of the folklore of American labor. Whatever its errors as to fact, "Paul Revere's Ride" is one of America's best historical ballads, not any too well known even by graduate students and upperclass collegians. And we have had need to remember it. We have need now to remember it, in the faith that

> borne on the night-wind of the Past,
> Through all our history, to the last,
> In the hour of darkness and peril and need,
> The people will waken and listen to hear
> The hurrying hoof-beats of that steed,
> And the midnight message of Paul Revere.

Of the other two members of "The New England Triumvirate," we have space for only a few illustrations. Oliver Wendell Holmes's use of folklore was in the tongue-in-cheek mode. "The Stethoscope Song, a Professional Ballad" (1848) and "The Deacon's Masterpiece" are *jeux d'esprit* using the ballad form and some ballad tricks to tell tall tales of a profession and a trade. "The

---

4. *Ibid.*

Ballad of the Oysterman" is a barefaced burlesque of the
balladeering of his friend Longfellow and others. Holmes
would have relished the fact that the folk have taken it
seriously, subjecting it to the perils of oral transmission,
and that it turns up in some American collections as a
"folksong!" "The Broomstick Train; or the Return of the
Witches" recalls a formidable amount of New England
superstitions and legends to account for the modern black
magic of the electric trolley car. The witches are brought
back with their broomsticks to pull the cars:

> As for the hag, you can't see her.
> But hark! you can hear her black cat's purr.
> And now and then, as a car goes by,
> You may catch a gleam from her wicked eye.

(In view of advances in modern urban transportation, one
wonders how soon electric trolley cars will seem to us as
quaint as witches riding broomsticks.) Holmes's friend
Lowell, who admired such "electrical tingles of hit after
hit," is significant for his artistic use of folk speech. *The
Biglow Papers* represents the cracker-barrel philosophy
applied to current national issues. The work is studded
with folk sayings like "I heern him a thrashin round like
a short-tailed bull in fli-time" and

> Tain't a knowin kind of cattle
> That is ketched with such moldy corn.

It has been noted that "The humor of Birdofredum, the
unmoral trickster and rascal, has deep origins in folklore
and appears often in the humor of the Southwest."[5] "The
Courtin' " is a lovely New England idyl in ballad form
and style.

---

5. Harold W. Thompson, "Humor," *Literary History of the United
States,* II, 736.

Walt Whitman declared, "I hear America singing, the varied carols I hear"—of mechanics, carpenters, masons, boatmen, shoemakers, wood-cutters, ploughboys, and housewives. Though he did not use the independent folk patterns, he is the Homer of the American folk, absorbing into his epic of self, in allusive form, the stuff of American folklore: "such folk references as the murder of the young men at Goliad, the Western turkeyshooting, coon-seekers going through the regions of the Red River, wooly-pates hoeing in the sugar field, the Missourian crossing the plains toting his wares and his cattle."[6] He records, as part of himself, his being

> At he-festivals, with black-guard jibes, ironical license,
>   bull-dances, drinking, laughter,
> At the cider-mill tasting the sweets of the brown mash,
>   sucking the juice through a straw,
> At apple-peelings wanting kisses for all the red fruit
>   I find,
> At musters, beach-parties, friendly bees,
>   huskings, house-raisings.

He works into his tapestry little ballad-like vignettes of such episodes as "an old-time sea-fight . . . as my grand-mother's father the sailor told it to me." Furthermore, his style is marked by such folk devices as the catalogue, parallel structure, incremental repetition, refrain, and folksong echoes like "It was good to gain the day" and "I will go back to Tennessee and never wander any more."

Author of one of the most eloquent tributes to the old ballads, Sidney Lanier wrote two fine imitations, "The Revenge of Hamish" and "A Ballad of Trees and the Master." His dialect pieces, such as "Uncle Jim's Baptist Revival" and "Thar's More in the Man than Thar Is in

---

6. Ernest E. Leisy, "Folklore in American Literature," *College English,* VIII (December 1946), 127.

the Land," though inferior, are closer to current American folksong.

With Bret Harte and John Hay, vernacular poetry in the United States plants its feet solidly on the ground of American folksong. Tickled by "Joe Bowers," they established the vogue of the Pike County ballad with such pieces as "The Heathen Chinee," "Jim Bludso," and "Little Britches." Shortly after this innovation, Irwin Russell, a young Mississippian, showed the possibility of a more authentic poetic treatment of Negro life and character than had hitherto appeared in pseudo-Negro poetry, even at its best in the songs of Stephen Collins Foster. Such poems as Russell's "Christmas Night in the Quarters" owed a part of their effectiveness to the undertones of Negro song and dance. Dialect verse exhibiting the inspiration of folksong and affinities with it constituted an important part of the local color movement. Among the chief practitioners were Will Carleton, James Whitcomb Riley, Eugene Field, and the Canadian Robert W. Service. Coming from the folk, Riley's stuff has gone back to the folk in surreptitiously circulated broadsides.

At the turn of the nineteenth century American scholars were busily collecting folklore and publishing it in more or less popular form. Child and Kittredge at Harvard and Kittredge's pupils were making the results of their labors available to the creative writers.

In the most successful twentieth-century poetry, folklore exploitation is seldom a program. The greatest exception is John S. Neihardt, whose two lays, "The Song of Three Friends" and "The Song of Hugh Glass," tell hero tales of the American fur trade. Though important, folklore for most contemporary poets is only one of many streams which the poet draws on for inspiration and creation. But its quieter simplicities and its creative power can be traced in much of the best that we read today.

Edwin Arlington Robinson used the ballad form in "Miniver Cheevy" and "Clavering," created authentic folk characters in "Isaac and Archibald," and used both the ballad form and some devices of ballad style in "Mr. Flood's Party." Edgar Lee Masters, though adapting form and technique suggested by *The Greek Anthology,* vividly realizes a whole gallery of folk characters, of whom "Fiddler Jones" is perhaps closest to a recognizable type:

> I ended up with forty acres;
> I ended up with a broken fiddle—
> And a broken laugh, and a thousand memories,
> And not a single regret.

Lucinda Matlock recalls the dances at Chandlerville, when in a change of partners at snap-out she "found Davis," with whom she was to live for seventy years, learning that "It takes life to love life." The humor of "Barney Hainsfeather" turns upon the mistake that occurred after the wreck of the excursion train to Peoria—

> John Allen . . . was sent to the Hebrew Cemetery
> At Chicago,
> And John for me, so I lie here.
> It was bad enough to run a clothing store in this town
> But to be buried here—*ach!*

Robert Frost has played with both folk material and form in such pieces as "Brown's Descent or the Willy-Nilly Slide," characterized by Louis Untermeyer as "a tart New England version of 'John Gilpin's Ride,'" and "Paul's Wife," a bit of apocryphal Bunyanana. To a folk proverb in circulation as early as 1856 Frost owes the most memorable line in "Mending Wall."

Nursed on *Uncle Remus,* Negro songs, and pioneer traditions, Vachel Lindsay reflected his heritage in such poems as "The Congo," "General Booth Enters into Heaven," "My Father Came from Kentucky," "The Statue

of Old Andrew Jackson," and "Preface to 'Bob Taylor's
Birthday.'" His "Bryan, Bryan, Bryan" derives one of its
most effective descriptive stanzas from a catalogue of real,
fabulous, and mythological American critters:

Oh, the longhorns from Texas,
The jay hawks from Kansas,
The plop-eyed bungaroo and giant giasiccus,
The varmint, chipmunk, bugaboo,
The horned-toad, prairie-dog and ballyhoo,
   . . . .
The farn, prodactyl and thing-amajig,
The rakaboor, the hellangone,
The whangdoodle, batfowl and pig
   . . . .
Against the way of Tubal Cain, too cunning for the young,
The longhorn calf, the buffalo, and wampus gave tongue.

Lindsay's "The Apple-Barrel of Johnny Appleseed" is a
vision of one of the few saints in American hagiology.

Carl Sandburg, singing minstrel, distinguished folksong
anthologist, skillful weaver of folk proverbs, owes little to
the forms but much to the feeling and the phrase of folk
poetry. Of old John Brown he wrote:

They said: You are the fool killer
     You for the booby hatch
     and a necktie party
      . . . .
They laid hands on him
And the fool killers had a laugh
And the necktie party was a go, by God.

Mr. Sandburg once told me that when he was young he
wrote many ballads in the folk style, and that in his
opinion this was the best sort of exercise to attain mastery
of poetic technique.

The best illustrations of the influence of all elements
are to be found in the poetry of Stephen Vincent Benét.
John Brown's Body begins with an "Invocation" that com-

plains of the attempts of previous poets who had sought
to capture the spirit of America and tell its stories in the
old molds and words.

> They tried to fit you with an English song
> And clip your speech into the English tale.
> But, even from the first, the words went wrong,
> The catbird pecked away the nightingale.
>
> . . . .
>
> Never the running stag, the gull at wing,
> The pure elixir, the American thing.

Of his poem the poet declares:

> This flesh was seeded from no foreign grain
> But Pennsylvania and Kentucky wheat,
> And it was soaked in California rain
> And five years tempered in New England sleet.

Recognizable grains of wheat are such folksong adapta-
tions as "Blow the Man Down," the spiritual "Oh Lordy
Je-sus," the lyric "Since I Was Begotten," the political
song of "Thirteen Sisters beside the Sea," "John Brown's
Prayer," snatches from "Dixie," "We'll Hang Jeff Davis
on a Sour-Apple Tree," recurrent lines from "Foggy Foggy
Dew," and dance tunes of Wingate Hall, the exquisite
ballad "Love came by from the river smoke," allusions to
"The Castle Thunder Men," Stonewall Jackson's dying
words, the "Jubilo" song "Sherman's buzzing along to the
sea," the various dialects of America, and a hundred anec-
dotes of the war as they were told by the fireside. These
and a thousand more details of the sort enrich the har-
monies and color the texture of *John Brown's Body*.
Among his shorter pieces, Benét's "The Ballad of William
Sycamore" is the incarnation of the pioneer spirit set to
a perfect American transposition of the old ballad music.
"The Mountain Whippoorwill . . . (A Georgia Romance)"
is a capital ballad on a fiddler's contest.

A glance at the work of poets still publishing or but recently dead shows a more oblique and sophisticated handling of folk elements. Wallace Stevens, in "The Comedian as the Letter C," begins:

> Nota: Man is the intelligence of the soil,
> The sovereign ghost.

Further:

> Nota: his soil is man's intelligence.
> That's better. That's worth crossing seas to find.

Thus:

> The man in Georgia walking among pines
> Should be pine-spokesman. The responsive man,
> Planting his pristine cores in Florida,
> Should prick thereof, not on the psaltery,
> But on the banjo's categorical gut,
> Tuck, tuck, while the flamingoes flapped his bays.

Thus, too, Stevens resorts to a folk saying to label the meaning of one of his most desolate and despairing poems —"No Possum, No Sop, No Taters." E. E. Cummings' " 'All in green went my love riding,' " without using the regular ballad stanza, recaptures, as did Keats and Scott in the traditional form, the glamor of the old chivalric world in the same way as, but more completely than, the ancient fairy ballads like "Tam Lin" and "Thomas Rymer and the Queen of Elfland." John Crowe Ransom's "Captain Carpenter" is a macabre *Don Quixote* in ballad measure, with phrasal echoes of "The Twa Corbies" and "Edward." This story of the slowly expendable but hardly educable idealist obtains a dash of its bitter irony from the simplicities of the old ballad. Hart Crane's "The Harbor Dawn" makes its nostalgia and its satire effective with "the sin and slogans of the years," There's no place like Booneville, though, Buddy," and "The myths of her fathers"—

As though the waters breathed that you might know
Memphis Johnny, Steamboat Bill, Missouri Joe,

and "Casey Jones" and "Deep River."

Two recent examples will indicate what is being done
with the local legend and the ballad. Phelps Putnam's
"Ballad of a Strange Thing" tells a story somewhat like
the old Pan and Syrinx myth, or, as Shelley told it,

> Singing how down the vale of Maenalus
> I pursued a maiden and clasped a reed.
> Gods and men, we are all deluded thus.
> It breaks in our bosom and then we bleed.

But the setting is New England, a bonfire with a ring of
cider-drunk Yankees listening to Jack Chance, a "lucid
fool" who has drifted "into the township of Pollard Mill"
to "sing his bawdy songs" and enchant "A dozen foolish
farmers." And the dénouement when autumn comes and

> From the black trees, choking the ditches
> And over the seas came sons-of-bitches
> With a hollow quarrel, the talking rats
> Of England and of Europe,

is as strange and remote in time as the girl's turning into
a "Shivering graceful sheaf of reeds." The ballad in "A
Strange Thing" moves into and out of the authentic setting as naturally as the grace notes on a fiddle.

The same casual, easy technique characterizes Robert
Penn Warren's "The Ballad of Billie Potts." Warren says
he heard the story "from an old lady who was a relative,"
and "The scene . . . was in the section of Western Kentucky known as 'Between the Rivers' . . . the Cumberland
and the Tennessee." It is a gruesome story of how a ras-
cally couple who keep a backwoods tavern and rob their
guests bring up a son to be a highwayman and unwittingly
murder him when, years after he has left home in disgrace,
he returns boasting of his swag and pretending to be a

stranger. The purely narrative part is told with the forth-
rightness and the brutality of the old murder ballads. But
into the simple tale the poet has infused the tragic irony
and frustration of man's life "on a doomed and derelict
planet":

You came, weary of greetings and the new friend's smile,
Weary in the art of the stranger, worn with your wanderer's
    wile,
Weary of innocence and the husks of Time,
Prodigal, back to the homeland of no-Time
To ask forgiveness and the patrimony of your crime.

Thus, material and form are only incidental and subordi-
nate to a deeply-realized meaning, as they doubtless were
to the Greek tragedians who told the old Oedipus story
of how a son killed a father.

These examples, I trust, are sufficient to establish my
thesis. From the beginning, folklore has been one of the
main ingredients of American poetry. First, it was used
in a conscious, conventional, somewhat decorative way,
in line with older precedents. Then, as Americans began
to think of themselves as Americans, and to feel the need
of a mythology, a legendry, and a tradition of their own,
they set about their task of inventing or adapting folklore
and incorporating it in a synthetic way—they made a cult
of it, with results of varying though on the whole inferior
merit. Meanwhile, scholars were gathering and publishing
American ballads, songs, and tales. It was only when creative artists steeped themselves in the living stream or
turned to it as an aspect of their own deeply-realized ex-
perience that they achieved complete and successful trans-
mutation. Folklore has been and will continue to be in-
dispensable to most poets, particularly to those who seek
to interpret us and our lives to ourselves. Chaucer stated
an old truth that he demonstrated in his own art:

> For oute of olde feldys, as men sey,
> Comyth all this newe corn from yere to yere,
> And out of old bokis in good fey,
> Comyth all this newe science that men lere.

As Thomas Mann makes Mai-Sachem, Joseph's wise old jailor, say: "There are, so far as I can see, two kinds of poetry; one springs from folk-simplicity, the other from the literary gift in essence. The second is undoubtedly the higher form. But in my view it cannot flourish cut off from the other, needing it as a plant needs soil."

FOLKSONGS IN FICTION

The close and organic connection between folk poetry and prose fiction is attested by the fact that the greatest of all folksong collections in our language, Francis James Child's *The English and Scottish Popular Ballads,* had its inception in Professor Child's desire to trace the evolution of prose fiction in English.

In 1936 I published in *The Sewanee Review* a long article embodying the results of my study of the use of folksong in fiction of the decade 1920-1930 describing the Southern scene. Since that time I have read a good deal of fiction about the South, for enjoyment rather than for critical study. Even so, I have noted that uses and practices characteristic of the 1920s have persisted. I have no reason to doubt that observations made then are valid for more recent fiction.

Time does not permit me to illustrate my subject now as fully as I did then. But I believe some account of the contents of my study will prove interesting.

A rather thorough inspection of fiction of the decade resulted in the finding of 25 novels and 22 short stories by distinguished or well-recognized writers that quoted folksongs as wholes or as tags. The 47 titles by 31 writers yielded 207 examples. After studying their use of folksongs, I wrote eighteen of the living writers, requesting permission to quote passages that interested me, and asking them for statements about their knowledge of folksongs and their opinions of the importance of folksong as a fictional resource. Fifteen replied, most of them at considerable length.

The stories showed four kinds of uses: (1) historical fiction using folksongs as bits of color or pictorial media appropriate to the settings and the characters—9 pieces of fiction containing 54 songs, in full, tags, or titles, or allusions; (2) fiction of contemporary life using folksongs as an important devices or material for describing characters and local color—31 titles, 116 songs; (3) fiction employing folksong as an essential thematic, structural, or atmospheric medium—8 titles, 37 songs; (4) fiction exhibiting the influence of special scholarly interest in folksong or theoretical knowledge of it—5 titles.

One of the finest historical novels about the South is Mary Johnston's *The Great Valley,* the story of a Scottish family that set out at the time of the Seven Years' War (1765) from Virginia, across the Blue Ridge, to their new home in the West. The old ballads are a part of the mental furniture of the sturdy but homesick Scots. Thus, when these pioneers pause at a point beyond Richmond, they see the new country as "a fairy world," and the child Elizabeth whispers, "That is belonging to the Queen of Fair Elfland, that Thomas Rymer rode with,

> 'Her skirt was o' the grass-green silk,
>   Her mantle o' the velvet fine,
> At ilka tett of her horse's mane
>   Hung fifty siller bells and nine. . . .' "

When "the grapevine had flowered six times since the crossing of the Blue Ridge," the family gather round the

hearth one cold November evening and listen to Elizabeth
sing "The Bonny Earl of Murray," father and mother
joining or commenting. On Elizabeth and Conant's wed-
ding journey, the lovers pause "by the two hills that the
Ulstermen had named Bessy Bell and Mary Gray" and
sing the old ballad of the two unfortunate lasses who
"bigget a bower" to escape a plague and died there. In
their log house Mother Dick sings, "in a cracked voice . . .
still sweet," the grand old ballad of Sir Patrick Spens.
Forest fires and Indian raids are discussed to the ominous
chorus of "Fire in the mountains"; Elizabeth's captivity
is preluded by "The Twa Sisters" and comforted by old
spirituals and "Hind Horn," the latter prophetic of escape.

Miss Johnston commented in part to me as follows:

Certainly folksong interests me. . . . In all my work if I have
not to hand the actual line or stanza that suits my purpose,
I invent it. . . . Sir Walter Scott's *Anon.*, in short. In *Croatan*,
for instance, [the two lullabies] are my own invention. . . . The
same applies throughout my work to snatches of Negro spirituals. Some are genuine—perhaps the most—but others ground
into me.

Broadly considered, the songs in these novels and short
stories are employed in the interest of historical realism.
They serve a purpose similar to that of notations on dress,
food, arms, customs, religious belief and feeling, political
events and opinions, and actual historical happenings.
They are, for the most part, songs that particular people
in the given settings could or would have sung. Some, for
example, as in Mary Johnston's *Croatan*, release an emo-
tion implicit in a given situation, or, as in the same author's *The Great Valley*, paint a natural scene. In books
by experienced story-tellers, emotions are usually evoked
or invoked in accordance with sound psychology. The
workings of mental association educe most of them. Only
a few emotional reactions—for example, one in *Croatan*—

seem to point to worked-up situations. On the other hand, to take an example from *The Great Valley,* many naturally suggest the mental equipment and habits of the characters. The "Hannibal Hane" ballad of old Bethel, which he has sung so long that he believes he is the composer of it, is a splendid instance, from *The Great Meadow* by Elizabeth Madox Roberts.

It is the deepening and broadening of the tendency of authors to make themselves a part of folklore that justifies separation of fiction of contemporary Southern life from historical fiction of the same region. Fiction being what it is and the practitioners often cultivating both types, there could be no marked differences in kind. Elizabeth Madox Roberts, for example, was the author of the historical novel *The Great Meadow,* about the settlement of Kentucky, and of such studies of life in the 1920s as *The Time of Man* and *My Heart and My Flesh.* The scenes depicted and the human nature delineated in all three are much the same. Indeed, the people of *The Great Meadow* are the ancestors of those in the other two novels, and Miss Roberts describes them in terms of first-hand knowledge of their descendants, using two songs traditionally current in her own family. But Miss Roberts and the other fictionists to be considered in this second group knew their people and their settings in time at first hand. Hence they are more able to penetrate beyond exteriors, to enter into the inner lives of their characters, to describe scenes in terms of a reality perceived and imaginatively assimilated rather than merely created out of data obtained from reading. Their material is stamped with the living images of the sources whence it springs. It is more thoroughly assimilated to American tradition.

The most interesting and artistic use of folksong is that which serves description of the inner, imaginative lives of the characters. Indeed, we often listen to a song hovering

in the subconscious and emerging only in phrases and
snatches, like the verbal substance of dreams.

The Time of Man is the story of a Kentucky family of
tenant farmers living in the latter half of the nineteenth
century. Ellen Chesser, sitting on a stone in the middle of
a creek bed, muses:

> And a story about a horse could talk and one about Fair
> Ellender, "O mother, O mother, come riddle my sport,/Come
> riddle it all as one./Must I go marry fair Ellender?" Ellender,
> that's me. And people a-dyin' for grief and people a-dyin' for
> sorrow. . . . I know a right smart o' pieces. . . .

Searching for a turkey hen which had failed to bring her
brood back to the pasture, Ellen began to sing a song she
had heard Ben sing:

> "Oh, little Blue Wing is a pretty thing
> All dressed out so fine.
> Her hair comes tumblin' down her back
> And the boys can't beat her time."

Continuing her walk, she slips into another song, a medley:

> Liddy Margaret died like it might be today,
> Like it might be today, like it might be today,
> And he saw the bones of a thousand men.

Later, at a party where she is a wallflower, she sees Jim
Townley, who plays the guitar, look at her. Suddenly she
is no longer sad about her torn shoes and her lonely nights.

> "I can sing a song." "Well, sing it," Mr. Townley said. "I
> can sing 'Lady Nancy Belle'—that's a story my mammy taught
> me a long time ago, one she learned offen her grannie. I can
> sing 'Lucy is a mighty Generous Lady'—whichever you'd rath-
> er." "Sing both." She sang—"Lord Lovel he stood by his
> castle wall."

The seven other genuine folksongs (dance or playparty
pieces, "Sourwood Mountain," "Joe Bowers," and a traditional version of the song that Burns worked into "Red,

Red Rose"), though perfectly adapted, are of more or less
extrinsic relation to Ellen's story.

A letter to me from Miss Ivor Roberts describes her
sister's practice as follows:

> The folk elements in the work of my sister, Miss Elizabeth
> Madox Roberts, are derived directly from the folk. Most of
> the songs mentioned or quoted were sung in my family. (The
> popular songs, especially *My Heart and My Flesh,* were heard
> on all sides at the time they were being sung.) Of the ballads
> . . . grandmother sang "Barbara Allan" and parts of the Lady
> Nancy Belle ballad. My sister used Josephine McGill's *Folk-
> songs of the Kentucky Mountains* to refresh her memory of
> the songs, but she used no song that was not heard either in
> her family or among the people about her.

In Sherwood Anderson's *Dark Laughter* John Stockton
runs away from his wife and goes for a cruise down the
Mississippi. Sitting in the shade of a tree by the river, he
hears Negro roustabouts:

> Oh, ma banjo dog,
> Oh, ho, my banjo dog,
> An' I ain't go'na give
> You none of ma jelly roll—

a song which is repeated elsewhere in the novel, with
variations. Mr. Anderson wrote me as follows:

> These ballets, folksongs, etc., are picked up in all sorts of
> odd places, and remain in the mind as old spots of color.
> Often, as you know, they reflect the sadness, longing, or
> gayety of people.
>
> But to a wanderer like myself—not a musician—and yet a
> man who does not take notes, it is hard to remember exact
> sources. It happens I do remember the source of the song
> "Banjo Dog." It sprang up among the Negro stevedores on
> the old steamer *Peerless,* on the service between Selma and
> Mobile, Alabama. I used to half live on the boats and the
> river. There was an old Negro woman who used to come to
> the landing and sell pies to the Negro levee men. She had a
> little dog named Banjo, and the workmen used to tease her by

threatening to steal the dog. One Negro would coax the dog away and others would imitate its barking. The song sprang up—"Oh, my banjo dog," etc.

There was more to the song that I do not remember.

Eight of the pieces of fiction chosen for study, besides making use of folksong for all the purposes hitherto described, employ folksong for even more essential and organic purposes: they use it to define the main theme, or to mark the plot structure, or to do both.

Of *The Quare Women, A Story of the Kentucky Mountains,* Lucy Furman wrote: "The atmosphere of this story, its background, and even many of its incidents, arise from the author's connection with the Hindman Settlement School, in Knott County, Kentucky. . . . The quare women come in from furrin parts and sot 'em up some cloth houses," preliminary to founding the school, and begin community health work. They import Isabel Gwynne, promptly dubbed "The Singin' Gal," from the Blue Grass, to assist in settlement singing.

Against a social background still feudal, in both the original and the Kentucky senses, with its ballad-singing Aunt Ailsie Pridemore and Fult Fallon, is set the love story of the Singin' Gal and the feud leader. Of the ten or more ballads described or sung (most of them sung, at length), with minute accounts of the manner of singing them and of the effects, the majority are used to motivate action or to mark the phases of plot. Fult and Isabel first become acquainted and mutually interested through an exchange of songs, including the former's "The Turkish Lady" and "Barbara Allan." To "The Turkish Lady" Isabel "listened, inexpressibly charmed. 'Do you realize . . . that that ballad goes way back to the Crusades?' " Later, Fult remarks, of Isabel's taste, " 'The older they are, the better she likes them—them old way-back ones that come over from old England and Scotland long time ago.' " He

sings her "Lady Isabel and the Elf Knight" because her
name "is in hit," and, in the words of the author, "many
another ancient ballad . . . forgotten by the more fortu-
nately placed, to become to the mountaineer, in his isola-
tion, the sole outlet for imagination and fancy, the chief
source of inspiration and ideals."

Soon, "Isabel felt as if, in his person, Romance itself
. . . was advancing swiftly toward her from the veils and
shadows of bygone centuries." Fult mistakes her feeling
for him and proceeds to woo her in accordance with his
"chief source of inspiration and ideals." In fact, he abducts
her, in good Young Lochinvar style, explaining and justi-
fying his action in terms of ballad logic. Reconciliation is
effected through a gorgeous ballad tableau entertainment
at the school—"scenes from the old ballads," to accompany
which "Fult sang the ballads," including "The Turkish
Lady," "Barbara Allan," "Jackaroo," and "Lord Lovel."
The total effect of *The Quare Women* closely resembles
that of ballad opera.

To a less extent, this is true also of the same author's
The Lonesome Road, which gets its title and its theme
from the song of that name, and uses stanzas to mark the
plot structure.

Two of Dorothy Scarborough's novels, *Can't Get a Red-
bird* and *The Wind,* illustrate the same principles. The
former, however, owes little more than theme and title
to the old playparty song. The latter is an elaborate ap-
plication of two songs to the telling of a story. Letitia
Mason, a Virginia girl, orphaned, comes to live with rela-
tives at Sweetwater, Texas, marries, and is driven to marital infidelity, murder, and madness by nostalgia and the
ceaseless wind of the plains. The meeting on a railroad
train between Letitia and Wirt Roddy, who is to be her
fate, is rendered ominous by his singing of the first stanzas
of "Bury Me Not on the Lone Prairie." Her first impres-

sion of the vast bleak spaces, the sand, and the wind re-
minds her of an old spiritual, "I run to the rock to hide
my face." These two songs, though there are others used
for atmosphere, bear the burden of mood and mark incit-
ing moment, climax, and catastrophe. The young wife kills
Roddy, finds "No hiding-place" for the body or herself,
and, in her madness, imagines she hears the corpse singing,
"But they buried him there on the lone prairie."

Olive Tilford Dargan's *Call Home the Heart*, exuberant
and beautiful story of third-decade life in western North
Carolina, makes partial use of songs as thematic and structural material. At least two pieces, one of great technical
value to the novel, appear to be original, composed in the
manner of folksong. The others are traditional. *Call Home
the Heart* tells of the lovemaking, marriage, toil, marital
infelicities, and eventual reconciliation of Britt and Ishma.
Both are distinguished singers in a singing community.
They make love in song, mark the rhythm of field labor
by song, play and sport to song, find their varied emotional
releases in song, and kiss and make up in song. The fine
dénouement scene is woven about a ballad spontaneously
composed and sung by their neighbors.

In several of the works already referred to in other connections, the authors' employment of ballads for fictional
purposes seems to be guided by some knowledge of ballad
history and theory. It is not the purpose of this study to
decide whether the knowledge is accurate or not. It will
be enough to show that such knowledge actually affects
technique.

The most elaborate and interesting example occurs in
Call Home the Heart. Ishma has deserted Britt, eloping
to a mill town with Rad Bailey. Preacher Siler has just
"churched" Ishma. Britt, having waited outside the church
during excommunication proceedings, invites Siler, no
mean fighting man, to unfrock himself. In the fist-and-

skull which follows, Britt wins, and the preacher loses both
the fight and his breeches. The sequel is best presented in
Mrs. Dargan's own words.

While Alec was heading the rescue, Si Welch called two or
three men apart—Si was the best ballit-maker . . . and the men
he singled out were good seconds. By the time the preacher
was gently picked up and set in Uncle Samuel Wayne's buggy
to be taken home, the ballit-makers had put something together that would do to begin with. . . . They set Britt on a
stump, and a circle was formed about him. "I'll sing the first
verse and chorus, sing it to 'Lovin' Babe.' Everybody knows
that tune. Whoever wants to can be makin' words up. . . ."
(Si was in such a tilt that he pitched into the next stanza
without waiting for the chorus.)

> The preacher lost his breeches, sirs,
>   An' Britt he lost his shirt.
> They soak in blood, they pound in mud,
>   But never they'll bite the dirt.

"Now," he said, "I want ever'-body here to make up lines
for this ballit an' git 'em to me by nex' Saturday night. We'll
meet at my house. But howsomever long . . . hit's goin' to end
this a way:

> An' Ishmar she was cryin' that night,
>   Cryin' to Red Bailee,
> 'I wish I's home with my ol' true boy,
>   A-sittin' on his knee.' "

To anyone with even an elementary knowledge of ballad theory, this episode is a full-blown example of communal composition. Every condition, every step in the
process, every feature of the result is present. Compare the
episode with George Lyman Kittredge's description.

A small tribal gathering, assembled . . . for the purpose of
celebrating some occasion of common interest. . . . The object
. . . is known to all. . . . There is unity of feeling and a common stock of ideas and traditions. The dancing and singing,
in which all share, are . . . closely related. . . . Here we have

the "folk" . . . a singing, dancing throng subjected as a unit
to a mental and emotional stimulus. . . .

Different members of the throng, one after another, may
chant each his verse, composed on the spur of the moment,
and the sum of these various contributions makes a song. This
is communal composition. . . .

Fiswoode Tarleton's "Curtains" is a story of hill-men
who made a "ballard" of "How High Sheriff Jett braved
twelve bad men" and were singing it while the Sheriff was
regaining consciousness from the effects of a wound. Here,
however, nothing is said about the actual process of composition, though it seems to be clearly implied, and the
"ballard" is certainly represented as being the product of
spontaneous folk composition. Such a fictional episode
seems improbable without the assumption of something
more than general knowledge, on the author's part, of the
theory of communal composition.

Further evidence of rather widespread acquaintance
with ballad scholarship by Southern writers can be presented only by allusion. Mary Johnston, James Boyd, and
Margaret Prescott Montague freely stated that they in-
vented folk-like songs. Dorothy Scarborough was the author of a fine scholarly work on folksongs. Rose Wilder
Lane wrote that she was the author of an unpublished
article on "The Ozarks Playparty." Elizabeth Madox Roberts freshened her memory of folksongs by consulting a
well-known collection. All of these connections imply
scholarly contact. The consequences are often self-evident.
Even in the fiction of those writers who expressly deny
semi-scholarly knowledge or critical interest it is evident
that their use of folksong and their consciousness of it
have been stirred by general information traceable to
scholarly work in the field. In the stories by those from
whom no self-furnished statement was obtained the strong
probability of scholarly influence is suggested.

A famous writer's feeling about my subject is expressed by Thomas Wolfe in a letter written to me on July 11, 1933. I quote part of it.

The reason your subject interests me is that songs of all kinds more than almost anything else, except odors, can evoke the memory of some lost or forgotten moment of childhood with a literal and blazing intensity that makes the whole thing live again. But these songs, I am afraid, are not folksongs but simply popular songs like "Has Anybody Here Seen Kelly," "Yip-I-addy-I-Ay," "Tammany," "Take Me Out to the Ball Game," "Love Me and the World Is Mine," "K-K-K-Katy," "Alexander's Rag Time Band," and so on. Many of them I am afraid are very trashy songs but able to make me live again some night in summer twenty or twenty-five years ago and hear the people talk on their porches, or my father's voice, and smell the earth, the honeysuckle vines, the geranium beds, and live, hear, and see everything again as nothing else on earth could do.

This is all I can write you for the present. If I had time and it would be of any interest or value to you I should be glad to tell you about many of these songs and the memories they evoke and the meaning they have for me, not only the popular song hits of the time but also all those scraps and fragments and chants of songs that children use—such as

> I asked my mother for fifteen cents
> To see the elephant jump the fence—

and that came from God knows where; but I am afraid none of these were folksongs, unless my understanding of a folksong is amiss. I wish I had known more of the songs you write about. What I have heard in recent years of the songs the mountain people sing makes me sorry that I missed it as a child. . . . I think [songs] have a tremendous evocative power in our memory of the past and of our own childhood, no matter where we come from.

The "Little Bird" in Mrs. Dargan's hired man's song "built its nest in nineteen places 'fore the song was done." Lest this study attempt to emulate that busy fowl, it must be brought to a close.

The use of 207 folksongs in forty-seven works of fiction descriptive of life in the South, by thirty-one different writers, among them some of the very best, is a basic fact that attests the importance of folk poetry as fictional material. The examples of this use have illustrated the variety and the organic quality of the media afforded by the songs: bright threads for the tapestry of history, elementary colors for genre painting of folk scenes, and character-revealing high-lights and shadows for the chiaroscuro of individual personality; thematic and choral music to suggest the moods and signalize the stages of dramatic action; and the spirit and substance of action itself. Specific practice and express statements from one-third of the writers represented furthermore bespeak an interest in folksong, sometimes scholarly and scientific, always intelligent and sympathetic. Judged in terms of its consequences in creative art, the work of scholars in the field of Southern folksong has not been barren of fruit.

As to further conclusions, again in the words of Mrs. Dargan's hired man, "it's 'lowable for the reader to put in more if he wants to an' can think of 'em."